Shift

Liv Jaimes

BookLeaf Publishing
India | USA | UK

Presentation by *BookLeaf Publishing*

Web: www.bookleafpub.com

E-mail: info@bookleafpub.com

ISBN: 9789358315653

First edition 2023

*To my mother, thank you for believing in
me.*

ACKNOWLEDGEMENT

I'd like to thank those who made this book possible. Thank you to BookLeaf Publishing, whose 21-day writing challenge has made this book a reality. Thank you to my parents, friends, and family for believing in me. Thank you, God, for the gift and passion for writing. And thank you reader for taking the time to read these words.

PREFACE

The inspiration for this book came from my own life while going through a season of change. The poems are words I badly needed to hear. I wrote this because I imagine that someone, somewhere, needs to hear these words as well. My hope is that these poems encourage you when you feel lost.

Cocoon

There is something to be said about becoming
No longer the you of yesterday
And not yet the you of tomorrow
When you are a song unfinished
A humming sound
A melody with no lyrics
Right on the precipice of something beautiful
Something new
Different
Better
Right on the precipice of you

Don't stop here.

Real life

I think I got tired
Of standing on the sidelines
A spectator only
Watching another live my dream
Tears welling in my eyes
While my heart trips, saying:
"I can do that too."
"I'm supposed to do that too."
I got tired of being in the desert
Thirsty
Dying for myself

Self Love

3

I hope that one day you will look in the mirror
and see the love in your own eyes.

Death...of a sort

No one talks about the phoenix that must die
We all want the glory found in rising from the ashes
No one talks about the pain of letting go of pieces of
yourself
The ugly, broken, hidden things we don't want seen
The parts that perished so we could live
No one asks the rose if the pruning hurts
We just glory in the beauty of its perfect form

These are the growing pains.

Hope Springs

Be hopeful for the you of tomorrow
In spite of the scars yesterday has given
In spite of heartbreak
In spite of madness
In spite of pain

The past has left bleeding wounds
But that's what hospitals are for
That's what healing is for

What joy it will be when your heart is whole again
Healed
Until then, may your fractured pieces still hope

Interlude

Rest.
You are striving so hard.
Don't you know?
Some things unfold on their own.

And yet...

We are still trying
Still striving
Walking towards tomorrow without a map
Our heart guiding us to places unknown
To places we cannot help but follow
"Where are you going?" they will ask.
"I will know when my heart says rest here" we will say.

Past,Present, Future

Don't give over to who they say you are
you are not the you of yesterday
You are not your mistakes

The past does not know the future

No Us

9

We have changed
Trying to grow together but we grow apart
like oil and water now
like a song out of rhythm
I used to love you madly
I used to call you first
Now I wonder if I should call you at all

Alive

Some days you will not have it in you
Some days it will just be you
Breathing in and then out
And that is ok

And so...

Breathe
Let the sun warm your skin
Know that it is ok to smile even when life is imperfect
It is ok to laugh
Ok to dance
Ok to have joy
Ok to become
Happy

Don't wait for the other shoe

Moving Forward

12

It's easy to stay here
When tomorrow is full of unanswered questions
When so much is unknown
When familiarity feels like safety
And comfort is a close friend

Press on anyway

Sabatoeur

Locked in this cage of my own making
With the key
Dying to escape
Afraid to be free
How silly
Silly
Silly of me

Shape-shifter

How to exist?
You have done it for other people
Transformed
Into whoever and whatever they wanted you to be
Until now

Now it's time to transform into you

How long

15

How long before you see yourself?
How long before you be yourself?
How long before you free yourself?

A Reminder

When all you see is darkness in front of you
When your days bring storms and rain clouds
Remember
Everything has a expiration date
Storms end
Darkness gives way to daylight
Tears turn to smiles

Just wait a while

Adolescence

You are growing
It will be awkward
You are changing
It will feel strange
New
Different
You will be a stranger to yourself at first
But you were never meant to stay the same your whole life through

Morning

Darkness gives way to dawn
The light shines on all of God's creation
Morning birds sing a new song
The day is for you
The day is for you
This day is for you

Flame

The fire came
and burned away
Everything
That could not stay
But you remain

Be Thankful

The pain did not destroy you
Instead, it has refined you
Brought you the gift of resilience
Imbued you with strength
You are still alive

A Butterfly's Purpose

21

Life will bring what it will
Still, you must fly

www.ingramcontent.com/pod-product-compliance
Lightning Source LLC
LaVergne TN
LVHW010858200726
843508LV00012B/2928